HALF-LIT HOUSES

Half-Lit Houses

Tina Chang

Four Way Books
New York City

Distributed by
University Press of New England
Hanover and London

Editorial Office
Four Way Books
POB 535, Village Station
New York, NY 10014
www.fourwaybooks.com

Library of Congress Catalogue Card Number: 2002116853

ISBN:978-1-884800-52-8

Cover art: *The Golden Days,* by Balthus. Hirshhorn Museum
and Sculpture Garden, Smithsonian Institution, Gift of the
Joseph H. Hirshhorn Foundation, 1966. Photographed by
Lee Stalsworth.

This book is manufactured in the United States of America
and printed on acid-free paper.

Four Way Books is a division of Friends of Writers, Inc.,
a Vermont-based not-for-profit organization. We are grateful
for the assistance we receive from individual donors and
private foundations.

Distributed by University Press of New England
One Court Street, Lebanon, NH 03766

Acknowledgments

Grateful acknowledgment is made to the editors of the following journals in which some of these poems originally appeared:

Asian Pacific American Journal: "Fish Story," "Seraphim"
Callaloo: "Ascension," "Invention," "Letter to a Stranger"
The Cream City Review: "Servitude"
Indiana Review: "Eleven, America and Spain"
Journal of the Asian American Renaissance: "Journal of the Diabetic Father"
Muse Apprentice Guild: "Ambient Flight," "To Do Harm," "Labor," "Episode"
Missouri Review: "Lessons in Sleeping," "Entrance, Exit," "Curriculum"
Ploughshares: "Origin & Ash"
Quarterly West: "Gou"
Shade: "The Burning," "Part of the Forest"
Sonora Review: "For"
Tamaqua: "Paradise," "Hearsay"

"Origin & Ash," "Invention," "Fish Story," "Journal of the Diabetic Father," and "Curriculum" are reprinted in *Asian American Poetry: The Next Generation*, ed. Victoria Chang (University of Illinois Press, 2004).

"Origin & Ash," "Labor," "Naming the Light," "Ascension," "The Burning" and "Invention" are reprinted in *Poetry 30: Thirtysomething American Poets* (MAMMOTH books, 2004).

My deep thanks to boni joi, Catherine Coy, Brian Komei Dempster, Timothy Liu, David Semanki, Glori Simmons, Tracy K. Smith and Barbara Tran for their wisdom and close reading of these poems. And the community of friendship which is indispensable to my life: Amy Brill, Nancy Bulalacao, Curtis Chin, Mark Ciecko, Adam Gazzaley, Lara Held, Judy Isikow, Jennifer Milich, Lara Rosenthal, Elly Wong and my friends at the Asian American Writers' Workshop. To Joel Clement for his many years of faith and belief when it was needed most. Special gratitude to Alberto Vitale and Dianne Lynch. I thank Nelson deDios for his inspiration and light. I'm also grateful to all of my teachers. And, of course, my appreciation to my family for patience.

A poetry fellowship from The New York Foundation for the Arts,
the Van Lier Fellowship, grants from the Ludwig Vogelstein Foundation,
and the Barbara Deming Memorial Fund as well as residencies from
The MacDowell Colony, Villa Montalvo, Fundación Valparaíso,
and the Vermont Studio Center were instrumental in the support of
this book. Thanks to Martha Rhodes for taking notice, and to Sally Ball
and Doug Goetsch for ushering this book to completion.

CONTENTS

III.

IV.

For my mother, Teresa
and her mother, Fu-Ying

I.

Every memory I have coveted and stolen.
Every minute I have recorded as if the night
would erase it from me. So I write on paper quickly
saying, This was my house. I once lived there.

Origin & Ash

Powder rises
from a compact, platters full of peppermints, a bowl of sour pudding.
A cup of milk before me tastes of melted almonds.

It is the story of the eve of my beginning. Gifts for me:

boxes of poppies, pocket knife, an elaborate necklace
made of ladybugs.

My skirt rushing north

There is something round and toothless about my dolls.

They have no faith. Their mouths, young muscle to cut me down.
        Their pupils, miniature bruises.

I hear the cries of horses, long faces famished, the night the barn burned.

      God and ashes everywhere.

Burnt pennies, I loved them, I could not catch them
in their copper rolling.

My mother's cigarette burns amber in a crystal glass.
I am in bed imagining great infernos.

Ashes skimming my deep lake.

The night the animals burned,
I kissed the servant with the salty lips.
There was a spectacular explosion, a sound

that severed the nerves, I was kind to that shaking. The horses,
the smell of them, like wet leaves, broken skin.

Laughing against a wall, my hair sweeps the windowsill,

thighs show themselves.

First came my body, my statue's back, then hair electric, matches
    falling everywhere.
Tucked in my pink canopy, I am plastic, worn cheeks grinning.

I found my little ones hiding from me, crying into their sleeves. They
    are really from a breeze,
momentary, white.

When we unburied the dolls, red ants were a fantasy
feeding on them, nest of veins, shrunken salted corpses.

There is mythology planted in my mouth which is like sin.
Keep fires inside yourself.
My mother once said, *When you were a baby, I let you swim in a basin of*
    water
until your lungs stopped. Since then, my eyes were open windows,

the year everything fell into them.

Cicadas hissing.

Ashes on my open book.

Ashes in mother's hair. Ashes on my baby brother.
The streets are arid, driven toward fire.

If I hurry, I will dance with my father before the sun sets,
my slippers clicking
on a thin layer of rain.

Invention

On an island, an open road
where an animal has been crushed
by something larger than itself.

It is mangled by four o'clock light, soul
sour-sweet, intestines flattened and raked
by the sun, eyes still savage.

This landscape of Taiwan looks like a body
black and blue. On its coastline mussels have cracked
their faces on rocks, clouds collapse

onto tiny houses, and just now a monsoon has begun.
It reminds me of a story my father told me:
He once made the earth not in seven days

but in one. His steely joints wielded lava and water
and mercy in great ionic perfection.
He began the world, hammering the length

of trees, trees like a war of families,
trees which fumbled for grand gesture.
The world began in an explosion of fever and rain.

He said, *Tina, your body came out floating.*
I was born in the middle of monsoon season,
palm trees tearing the tin roofs.

Now as I wander to the center of the island
no one will speak to me. My dialect left somewhere
in his pocket, in a nursery book,

a language of child's play. Everything unfurls
in pictures: soil is washed from the soles of feet, a woman
runs toward her weeping son, chicken bones float

in a pot full of dirty water.
I return to the animal on the road.
When I stoop to look at it,

smells of trash, rotting vegetation,
the pitiful tongue, claws curled tight
to its heart; eyes open, eyes open.

When the world began in the small factory
of my father's imagination, he never spoke
of this gnarled concoction of bone and blood

that is nothing like wonder but just the opposite,
something simply ravaged. He would die soon
after the making of the world. I would go on waking,

sexing, mimicking enemies. I would go on coaxed
by gravity and hard science. While he rested in the satin
of his shriveled skin. Eyes swollen to exquisite planets.

My Father Dreams

He is shrinking by degrees
but no one is counting.

To the East, fishermen cast nets
over his children. To the West,
rocks fill up his wife's shoes.
She will never walk again.

Even when he is standing
like a headless nail, a battered fish,
he refuses all the food that is given him.

His bones have made islands of themselves.
The soul begins to speak:
spoon, ladle, malice in his mouth.
The body, a cage. Sundown.

His fingers fall away from his face.
One day he will wander away
from home and will not recognize
anyone who tries to stop him.

Three weeks later he will come home
from rain dying of fever.
But he will die of hunger first.

Fish Story

It is the hour of news. The television cracks
its voice over the radiator and the blue carpet. Always
that same cooked silver of you, oil spilling
from the mouth, ginger and scallions burning

through the scales. My father thinks you are delicate
as he steals the eggs from the purse
of your belly, white interior exposed and steaming.
I think of you breathing before the slipping out.

You once slept on a bed of cracked shells.
Jellyfish swelled around your eyes. Your body weaved
through coral. Cold blood stained the air when you were caught,
the snails and the clouds erasing. Netting grasped

the whole of you, the back bending so completely,
it could snap as water escaped your yellow heart.
Rubber tires and shrimp, green glass and mollusks
were caged with you. I know how painful it can all be:

the blade and the quick gutting,
the aroma of yourself frying in a smoky haze,
your body covered with radishes and leafy greens.
This activity of eating brains is real.

The knowledge of abalone, barracuda, the stingray
can be transferred by licking the flowers
from inside the skull of a fish. The bowl of the sea
and all its blue water, amphibians, salty mammals

can be absorbed in one swallow. And so my father does this
with hope. As his sight diminishes he pushes
out your eyes with his thumb;
you see the dry, contained world in this white

room before he sucks you down. This is the last
of the swimming, the final melting of fin and gills,
life broken down by the sallow tongue and feverish saliva,
the salt and sauce defeating you.

Versions

It is the middle of January
in the year I am trying to remember.
I'm in a small red jacket with
mittens clipped to sleeves.
The mittens are attachment
which means the father never left.
My stained lips breathe a white haze.

Now my brother is laughing,
but maybe he is screaming
and I must reach him through
the snow. He is sitting beneath
a willow tree, holding his wounded leg
and there is no one to help him.

My mother is inside believing
in safety as she puts bones into broth.
She has all the makings of a mother
but in another version she throws
everything into the refrigerator
and forgets.

I am fatherless which means
the father is in another room,
hiding where no one else but myself
can see. This game of hide and seek
when I am a girl is dangerous.
The fact that I've studied the weather
tells me the snow never stops.

The tiny hearts of strawberries
go frosted with rot.

Accident of Trees

My stepfather tells me my place is a doghouse.

Nothing left of wood, of money, of food.

I think of the judgment of my best friend's

father who aches with a grief. A silent one.

A tapping of his fingers on the table.

A tap, tap, tap for every one of her failures,

the sound of pigeons taking flight from

their cement nesting. Which is better?

The heart that is an organ of vengeful ambition

or the one that sits motionless like a boulder,

a year about to die? The sun swings from

a spool of orange thread. The grass gone

a caramel shade of green. It is beyond me.

This unexpected, wicked beauty.

Today I have no answers. I know nothing.

It is a blessing to own this, to have no wonder.

Lessons in Sleeping

I.

I once knew a narcoleptic girl who sat at her desk
head propped on elbows sleeping while chalk
scratched heavily on the blackboard.

I watched the globes
of her eyeballs travel the length
of her past and back again. I watched her

slumber through arithmetic. I envied
the miles she traveled and how she responded
when the recess bell rang.

How she awoke and ran,
heels clicking on marble,
her ribbons flying.

II.

Sleep where you find yourself standing.
Bend your knees, tilt the head.
Think of all the things that make you weary:

your mother, the boulevard, politics.
The dozen eggs that dropped this morning,
the knife that refuses to gleam.

Lean back, use a wall to steady yourself.
Forget the lessons the buildings have taught you
of heat and brick and noise. Imagine the sound

of your mother calling you from the yard.
You are inside. It's the middle of August.
How you could concentrate on nothing

but the erratic motion of mosquitoes.
Their love of the moist season, the bed
of your scented skin.

Think of the children that will be born
unto you and all the days
you will be deprived of sleep.

The jugular moves, arms collapse to the sides,
and the eyelids,
the weight of two bodies falling in water.

III.

There were trips I took as a girl:
my mother, my brother and I
in a blue Pinto, shining its way

to the Grand Canyon, Muir Woods,
Niagara Falls. The convenient meals falling on vinyl,
the sun dropping on the hood of the car,

my brother and I dreaming
of motion as we slept.
Yes, that dream was a good one,

the one about the house
that remade itself over and over again.
I walked through it feeling comfort although

I never lived there. If I tried to wake up,
it only pulled me in further.
And the roads were filled with the threat of snow

but it never snowed. My mother continued
her drive and some kind of wind
seeped through the window and hovered

in the dream, gliding down a staircase,
shaking the fern leaves, blowing the screen door
open like a bomb.

IV.

The pillow is a soft instrument invented for the head.
You place it there: a bright fragile egg,
a hand, a mouth wide open for air.

A mattress beneath you
keeps you from wandering.
The blankets secure you in place.

The evening sounds can be hazardous:
your brothers cursing in the barren streets,
static television, dinner bowls thrown away.

V.

In the well of sleep, there is a ladder
which brings you from one layer of slumber
to the next: *Prairie, aerial, nimbus, tomb.*

You are a misfit or a starlet. Your decision
to stay or go depends on the temperature,
rapture, or the stranger who touches you

and coaxes you to rest a bit longer.
And your heart stops when the world
is on the brink of rain.

VI.

Fairy tales are premonitions
of what can really happen.
A beautiful child finds out she is a woman

by morning when the birds
wake her and there is blood on the sheets.
A boy finds the story

that frightened him persists
in daylight. Bits of it like hair erupting
on his soft chest.

VII.

I am sitting on a checkered blanket.
The sun hangs above me on a string.
My father is planting tulip bulbs

in my honor. The girl is so entranced
by her father who holds light
in his tattered garden gloves.

Then there is the waking and the feeling after that.

Entrance, Exit

In the cycle of birth and death, sentient beings cannot be independent....
　　　　　　　　　　　　　　　　　　　　　　　　—Yin Shun

It is 1954 and I'm lost.

A servant has told me
that I am a queen
and I will drown.
All around me,
puddles I'd like to touch
because they remind me
of someone I've forgotten.
They multiply into oceans.
My dress parachutes lemon.

My face immaculate with water.

Water turns to snow.
Walking to the store,
everything covered
in fresh powder,
the entire town sinking.
My home is buried
beneath frost. I cover
my mouth as snow

hovers, a swarm of bees.

Chalk dust eddies.
I am a twelve-year-old boy

who has found
a bruise on my leg.
The bruise is shine, indigo.
My teacher calls my name.
and I raise my hand.
Outside, three boys
press their faces to the window.
They will wait for me
in a field, laughing

boxing their pig shadows.

When I tell lies
I think of my brother
in the hospital.
His ailing weakens me,
his illness terminal.
I once glimpsed a woman
eating blackberries
on her fire escape.
It was summer;

she had nowhere to go.

I have lost my keys.
I search beneath a purple scarf,
behind blue perfume bottles
given to me for my seventieth birthday.
I remember something I buried
in the backyard of my childhood home.
I call everyone to tell them

I will die tomorrow.
As I close my eyes, I hold tightly

to the keys that I have just found.

My mother smiles
at my newborn limbs, the sun
lights her dress from behind.
Applesauce dries to a crust
in a bowl. A door slams
and my father rushes with arms
larger than my atmosphere.
I cry until my lungs give out.
I cry until the landscape dissolves,
and I can do nothing but rest
until the next moment
when I find my body
placed in the world again.

Blueprint

I sleepwalk in a dress the color of bone,
amidst the lushness of curtain and rug.

There is the danger of slipping
into grains of evening. Follicles

of hair pepper the sinks and linens.
I take hold of the arm of a banister when

my mother's mouth lets go a sound, hung over
all the pictures of the house. She is crazy

because she wants quiet. Her voice could
throw toasters or melon knives. The spatula

makes us sit, the fork makes us tender
in the heart. When there is not enough water

to bathe in, I sit in the sink waiting.
The dried bees are still clinging to the screen

in the bathroom. My mother is in the bedroom
swaying to the music of sheets being folded

in her arms. She collapses after the old song is over.
My brother is in the garden again pulling

dandelions back by their lovely, lost faces.

II.

Of the woman I once saw, flailing in a river,
I gently sew the outlines of her,
crossing the dirt falling on her own image,
body dragging splinters of water.

Servitude

Li Sau and Li Jie   [Hunan, 1938]

She takes one breast out of her silken undershirt
like a secret, a warm brown egg and places it into his
open mouth. His body is hammocked

in floral cloth, tied to her bosom. August sweats
at the base of her neck. She gives away
her milk to a child she calls *shiou an,* smallest

night. She wishes he were her own as she crouches
in a field separating rotted stems from dried tea leaves.
I think of unraveling her two long

braids when I do the chores—chasing the crazed
chickens with their throats cut, stringing them by their feet
to the front trees. Bodies dripping

with leaves, the air smells of wild blood everywhere.
Tonight, after she has swept crickets down the back steps,
after I have washed dung from my fingernails with ginger

she will come quietly. We will lie down
on woven straw mats and watch the hanging
branches scrape against the unarmed sky.

She puts her fingers to my lips. I smell
smashed guava and lilac powder. I eat what she
brings me: bits of pig knuckle and mushrooms

collapsed in brown sauce. The whole town is strewn
with horses and red doorways and burned fish.
Past this house, there is a field set afire.

The torching of it like a lit city.
Li Sau, the bruised night pours in through all
the shutters of the house and nothing is coming for us.

Hunger
[Hunan, 1940]

There is a city called Hunan
where she opens her arm with a knife.
The blade sings of pavement,
of wall, of the place on her bicep
where it will carve out some young muscle.

When she cuts, she does not feel
the blade as vendors chop wide-eyed
fish heads from their epileptic bodies.

Her blood rushes out like a shower
of tiger lily. Then she covers her arm
with a palmful of coal. Years later,
the cradle of her arm is shrunken,
fading back. The gutter of her skin
tells of epidemics, hysteria.

When the knife was resting on a shelf,
she carried the diamond of flesh
to her grandfather and told him to eat it
so the sickness would release him.
He died that evening as she sat
holding the image of herself unraveling.

Minutes before his departure,
she made him swallow it whole
the part where the knife had severed
the nerves and taken away a bit of her.
Merely populating the minutes,
there was just a bit of sky left.
And the moon was just a pest,
a flicker.

Siren

The darkness holds her quivering
like a girl leaning over a boat.
The ripple of water and light
fool her into believing.
Light penetrates water
and makes folds in places
the wind may have overlooked.

In my world, I never swim,
only will myself to be the one
who is foolish enough to want
to touch the light on water,
where desire follows me
and wraps its arms around
me, body hitting water.

Kneeling

As she walks down the basement steps
to see what it was she was entering, her heart pleads,
tell me a story. The body leans as if to listen.

Children run along the pavement in the last weeks
of summer. The body is puzzle and memory,
pieces that lock together, without logic, without magic.

The father takes a handful of rice grains and scatters
them onto the basement floor. The girl is asked to kneel.
The grains press into her knees which begins

a small punishment. Her thin frame is made thinner
by shadows when the door closes and she is left in darkness.
She hears her brothers upstairs in their rooms, laughing

in their bright windows. She hears children outside
tapping a drumbeat with their frantic running.
It is the story of a girl kneeling in the darkness.

And if we ask her to tell it, she will tell it differently.
She would say the body is not a puzzle but an anchor
cast into an ocean. She would say that she was not afraid

but weary and bowed her head letting darkness
surround her like a wilderness. The rice breaks open
like tiny flowers, blooming into blisters.

For hours, the body surrounded by darkness
becomes the darkness, and there a chasm grows,
deeper and wider, separating until she cleaved

into twin girls: the one who breathed inside
that small space and the one who grew
a secret language. Nothing like praying

but something hard won, like balancing
on a thin wall, uncertain which way gravity
would bring her, memory teetering on a question mark.

The door opens with a light that makes her eyes
tighten. She rises from her place. She is flying.
She tears at her arms until she alights.

Impossible Rapture

When the barn doors close,
the woman with the tiny hands
pets the cow with sorrowful eyes.
The hay beneath her in heaps,
she falls to the ground.

Outside the fireflies are hungry.
They circle around a lantern, feast
on the last bit of moonlight.
The sound of everything larger
than she's ever heard but more
brilliant, more hurtful. She hears
birds although there aren't any.

The tree and her voice sing.

The body relaxes inside.
A branch moves, she is asleep.
Her body is so small like
the heroine who made it
through her life, long enough
to tell about it.

Giving the Girl
[Hunan, 1942]

Born, I wrapped you
in deep blue and sewed
a sickness in your throat.

I gave you away
to a farmer who trained
you to be his son.

These skies disappear
and my arms one world
lighter.

This heaviness crushes
me to pieces. Absence.
A door swings to shut its shadow.

Your brothers are
a terrain as untouchable
as birds.

Dark haired boys
hiding behind my legs,
two white trees.

I am whispering
a story to myself
I would have told you.

You visit me in dreams,
sit in me and ask me
why I am lost.

Outside, there is
a whole plantation
made of your face.

The sound of simmering,
your voice calling me.
Miles and miles.

Your father lies on top of me
nightly and presses me closer
to the base of the house.

To Do Harm

The life I longed for was a great white wasp, fluttering above me
    its transparent nerves hushing an important silence.
The tree that stares out at me with its future going extinct.
    The land bleeds with a kind of bleeding that signals growth.
I wake up each morning with marks on my flesh, scratch-marks
    that are human and alien, as if the woman in the middle of the night
didn't participate, didn't open herself to a more hurtful mystery.

Famine
[Hunan, 1932]

Mother explains her love of heat
as she stirs over a burned pan.

We collect them one by one:
beetle, ant, june bug, roach, gnat, firefly.

The cow crumbles on its thin legs.
And the dust over a million eyes.

We let go of a handful. Tiny black legs
spinning on a mound of sugar.

Let us eat, thankful for the small things
that wander by the window or a door.

We grasp what flits by us, flashing.

Hearsay
[Hunan, 1943]

So little wind to go around.
The whole family sleeps on bamboo mats.
Their eyelids yield, flicker shut
like broken light bulbs.

Mosquitoes burn a hole in your skin
to take blood. There are no clocks
to tell the time. And tell me the part
that I hope is not true:

How your brother reaches toward you
as he would for bread because the supper
is not enough. You are beautiful,
becoming a round thing and he yearns

to touch your belly. He reaches to enter you,
you can not decipher copper pots from his face,
you want to run or sound out, but you count
the heads of your younger brothers and sisters.

Count their breathing. Had there been
more food, had the night been a cool plate
of something else to offer,
there would never be this hunger.

Mother, I will be born in fifteen years.
And after that I will hear
the voices of my family recounting
our history. *We come from a dynasty*

of vanity and ruin, says one uncle.
We are here like fig trees, to tend
to our own solitude, says another.
I have stopped listening.

Gou

In the rain, the sound of them
housing themselves under bridges.

Their bones fall to one knee,
then the other. The dogs think:

*thick lather of ocean, something
to smother hunger.* A hand palmside up,

offered a bit of salvation. In the constant
dream, teeth tear into my arms. Teeth

fall to the ground like coins. The father
that died is the patron saint of animals

that guard, that wander, that obey,
that creep, that bleed.

Paradise
[Hunan, 1944]

The men will not be back.
I stay and love my reflection in the pot
or imagine myself in the white stones
at the bottom of the river.
I place them in my pockets today.
Watch me drown.

The village of women put up talismans
by their front doors: pig, dog, a crazed monkey.
Keep us from becoming savages.
They hang miniatures upside down
by the feet, by the neck.
It rains for two months.

We tend ourselves like gardens:
brush our hair to a blue-black sheen,
scrub our teeth with the nubs of our fingers,
carry children heavier by the day.
In the eighth month,
we all give birth to girls.

Missionaries have given us hymn books.
I hold one close to my bloated lungs.
My little girl is good with the soil. She will be
a farmer, a priest, a constellation.
Through the cypress grove, our feet sink
into black mud, we lose the children

who have wandered. Their laughter strips
the trees. Night comes over us
in the form of ravens. Rifles

have been strapped to us. Haze settles.
Starlight, infant hands, open lips.
The midsummer evenings chill me.

At night, we follow one another
in straight lines. We hold each other by the waist,
humming as we wade into the river. Airplanes pass
overhead. We kiss. Our dresses have imprints
of white leaves falling from nowhere,
from no visible branches, no forest of trees.

Libretto
[New York, 2000]

An empire falls to a smoldering seed.
A voice fades from it. Pastries: little
purses of custard, red bean, a bit of mud.
The rotten city where smoke flowers
from her face, her lungs etched
in perfume. Shop signs: Chinese characters
contained in squares, the moon fixed
into a picture, strange glass she looks
into, angled little bones.

Notes On Longing

It smells of after-rain tonight.
Duck bones, a wounded egg on rice.
On the corner, there is a shop
that makes keys, keys that open
human doors, doors that lead
to rooms that hold families
of four or seven who sit at a table.
There is a mother who brings
sizzling flounder on a wide platter
for the family whose ordinary
mouths have been made to sing.

III.

My hands wind themselves around
a crystal glass, that shrill melody playing
over my throat again. Everything
like the tongue, a fresh animal.

Labor

The bodies are fools for loving each other's
empty cavities. A hollow stick leans against
the wall in the dark. You love her foolishly
despite your will. Because things will ruin and ruin.

When the silence is something larger and louder
than the thunder tearing over the house, when
the field seems emptier because she stands
at its center. When the body doesn't feel

like it's yours, you offer it. Then
everything stops like the end of a story,
a film on the edge of breaking. House of spun sugar
threatens to burst at its hinges, snow falls

in music sheets, table letters remain half written,
coins scattered across the room. Outside,
crows take off shattering the thick of rain.
And the work of rain becomes harder.

Vanity

A wasp crawls over the shadow of two people.
The woman pins, repins her hair. The wet tendrils a dark arrow
pointing to her lower spine. Yellow flowers fall
when a man slips his hands over her stomach. She parts
a little, paints her mouth, a wild bird in the doorway.
She puckers her lips, two hushed waves.

∿

Mandarin oranges, halved and sitting by the window.
She demands. Her dress blooming as she turns.
He gives her a drawing, a blue sheet of paper
sewn with invisible stitch. He has attached birds
to everything. She ignores him and eats the orange,
juices dripping down her arm. She looks at the drawing
and knows that love exists in her tundra, her arctic
swelling. His kind of love: windblown, impoverished.

∿

In front of her, a paper boat melts into the water's
interior. She sees the season, now, in pieces. A hand
against the sky as if about to touch its distance.
Grass giving way to more grass. She's lost in the green.
She hears a parade made of one cymbal, a child's drum,
and one woman's trembling song, a lost octave only she
can hear. She runs to the balcony but no one comes.

∿

She looks at her face on the back of a spoon, fixes
her eye on the eye that looks back, touches the silver
as if disrupting the surface of water. She puts the spoon
down, her body moving now toward the person waiting
for her. She lowers the strap of her dress. Pigeons dive,
making a collective shadow inside her.

Curriculum

1: Prowess

Walk into a room a high priestess.
Inherit fortune through the mouth.
Feel God's hand reaching down
to place a gift on your tongue
like a fresh coin. Swallow.
This is how you take it: bread, light,
a vantage point in the heart.

2: Stamina

Keep going when lungs are shriveled,
two bags of bad air. The professor sleeps
in a suit, makes ready with a suitcase
by the door and a wife
at his elbow. Wake up early,
wake up dying.

3: Render

A young girl brushes her hair
till she aches. Her father stole a chicken from a neighbor.
As punishment the town priest takes
the daughter as his slave. Every night he pushes
the curtains back. He forgives and is forgiven.

4: Contempt

The heart is daily slain.
The man is happy who goes off
to war, kills fields full of children,
becomes a hero. He returns, axing
the thin white flowers of his walls.
Then offers himself to his family,
quietly, an earful of bullets.

5: Change

I was once a gnat, then a gardener,
then a fallen saint. Each time I am new again,
failing by flying, then
by drowning. The nuns waft by
in their habits whispering of the criminal
who got it real good. My skin is molting,
an inky blue. When I shed, I come out clean.

2075: Let go.

Someone somewhere is sharpening a pencil.
I have taught myself the good lesson.
You are the sin of the imperfect,
the most wretched one, the face I long for.
The teacher notes his students on a page,
their attendance in red ink, marking presence,
marking loss. The savior builds faith
in a ruined church. Touches you
with water and with fire.

Part of the Forest

It's the devil you would like to extinguish.
The one that is hiding in the still life between
the bright yellow pear and the claw of a bird.
It makes the painting deteriorate before it's finished.
The baroque angels are sinking on top of you.

Lower. And the temperature drops. Your mouth
is a wrinkled heart, twice deflated, ear pressed
to the floor. Someone is laughing next door.
The bell rings. You put your arms around
the messenger, make love to him by the doorway.

A flower appears in the hollow space
you carved with your silence and regret.
The devil pushes the girl's hair behind her small ear.
You can hear his music. You might know the song.
The words in your mouth taste like sugar, gun powder.

You're alarmed at the darkness, in the rib cage
where the heart beats like a spent ember. Perhaps
it was the damaged liver, the guilty splayed interior,
pink once you halve the organ. When everything
is lit on fire, you say the organ died.

Eleven, America and Spain

There was a wake for the relative
you didn't know. Food arranged neatly.
Little Japanese packages wrapped
in scented paper, a hand-held camera
to record the weeping.

The letters written to you were folded
into origami cranes, pressed into
your small palms. Just the thought
of the alphabet now. The dead's
correspondence, something of flight,
the persistence of wind devoid of winter.

Your swing attached to the tree sways
from its own motion. There is the slow
tilting left of the man who may fall asleep
into the pages of his tattered bible.

&

Two months before, you stared at a girl
outside of the bullring in Spain. Her little fits,
outbursts. So much like yourself. The girl's dress
was ruffled pink hysteria. Gliding across the ground,
she was puddle-stained, goddess, half-grown, floral.

Baby señorita, you thought to yourself.
Gold rings weighed down her fingers.
Perfumed, she was led into the arena by her father.
King of the Gypsies with a face of a ruined cave,
a cane in his other hand, a head of a wolf at its tip.

&

In America, all you can think of is your first kiss
or perhaps the last breath of your grandmother.
The old woman sits in a chair, her heart a balloon
rising up. A small stringed instrument plays its last music.

When the black blood flowed from the bull's
fallen body, a boy reached to give you
a deep probing kiss, the tongue made its way
to the center. The bull's ear was cut off at dawn
while an entire nation cheered, the little girl clapped with joy.

Your grandmother lifts herself to walk to a metal fence
to keep it slightly ajar. She tastes a word filling her
in Chinese and struggles to replicate it in English.
A Spanish song plays in the streets. She has opened
the metal fence for the last time and for no one in particular.

The Unpainted Mouth

The birds are perfect in the way
they are constant. Song in the morning,
another sound responding. I am guilty
of folding the world into a fan,
the shape of which collapses

and then opens with its wide opulence,
forcing the wind to take everything away
with it. What engine of what bright animal
drives me forward? I dream that it is summer.
My skirt skims my knees. Sunlight

has finally made it through to melt
the soiled frost. Last night, from thousands
of miles away, you dreamt of me.
Watch how a night so dark could gather us
into its skirt. How driven I've become.

Afraid to lose the beauty I never owned,
afraid to fail. Today we boil water and place
one egg in. We watch it work into a frothy
yellow heart and we eat it together.
I love you beyond our poverty.

You wake in the morning with me,
brush my hair and go back to sleep.
Japanese blossoms bloom from one thin
branch. It sways. You shift too.
What we have in this life

is neither passed through a kiss
nor is it anything like food
but a desire so great
we swallow it whole.

What the Dead Say

When I am in a building that is collapsing, I try to hold you
in the same place, but you slip away from me, call my name
three times, then we are just rubble. The next day we are
walking together as if nothing happened, nothing indicating
tragedy except that you are speaking with an accent of the dead,
a soft lilt like Italian except higher and higher as if you must
reach me somewhere else. The bee flies out to land
on a cut lemon, the fruit's dry universe still a house.
It is difficult to comprehend. The snow will fall soon.
And swiftly.

Seraphim

I.

There is a man lying in her bed.
His mouth a broken peanut shell.
She unbuttons her nightgown
and tells him to breathe.

Down in the cellar of her mind
it is exactly 34 degrees. Rain outside.
She runs her fingernail along his wrists,
his temples. On the porch, her mother sits
and pens a letter. Lightening splits the sky
in two.

II.

On the eve of her eighteenth birthday,
she was not thinking of dinner
nor the violet circle on her back
that formed a perfect O on her skin.
She thought of the cold that plagued her feet.
She read that cayenne pepper warms the soles.
Remedies. She wondered what she could still believe in.

III.

She once believed the song of angels
was the sound of a woman
releasing a high-pitched cry

into her lover's ear.
When the angels heard, they came
and beat her with their outstretched wings.

They don't speak
of such things in heaven.
This is memory: their feathered
wings descending upon her each time
she heard the trees whipping
the naked wind.

IV.

At certain hours of the day when he phoned her,
she imagined sad steel trains leaving his eyes.
She questioned her daily gestures: opening the mail,
adjusting the sleeve of her dress. Her hands, the piles
of laundry, the high windows all became ugly. The radiator
was a putrid silver. She could be no one else but herself.

V.

When she was twelve she received communion
in a chapel that seated twelve. Christ looked on,
his eyes two stones. Body. Blood. Her fingers
still smelled of her violet part. She was dressed in white
and there was a rip in her stocking as fine as a crack in the world.

VI.

I will never know what God intends for me.
A dog rests its head on my ankle. The city sinks
into a cup of water. "Spanish Harlem" rises to a window
above me. The vendor continues to sell sour oranges
by the dozen. The child is grown. It eats. It grows.
It is December now and I am an ordinary girl.

IV.

These are the last remnants of the world.
Every kind of love I was blind to while I lived.
He is waiting by the porch light.
Mosquitoes pierce the lightbulb's naked blue.
The stars let go the sky that housed them.

Half-Lit House

There is the affliction of trees,
an icy music tangled in the branches
limbs cutting a movement, half-dancing

half-stabbing a shadow in the barren.
Rivulets of my voice hanging,
a notion.

Outside: bark, burr, fig, seasons crosshatched.
Inside: lantern, rodent, blood cells killing their kind.
Further in, half-eclipsed, half-lit,

a figure is propped in a chair, left in the manner
in which he was choking. Light of refrigerator.
The child is weeping, her own ghost more

singular than the wind that blows through them.
In the bedroom, an aged woman, her hair,
froth of sea gone mad. A candle lights

the pale interior of her skull. What she remembers
is driving her back. In her caravan, her footmen
push through the grasses. Figurines watch

as her scarlet silk molds to the shape of a century.
They have no names, but we can tell their genus
by the relics they've left: toppled statues

of the conquered, invisible coins spent
on parched waters, garments sullen
with ambition. They have eaten without food.

By the window I cut a dim picture
with the tip of my finger. In the cellar
a shrine of oranges, so incomplete in their

roundness, photos of the dead caught
in still desolation. I move through them,
half-bitten curtains, half-lit,

touch the toppled roof beams. Leaving, left.
Abandoned archway, I step outside
to view the house from another province.

Insomniac, never the adequate hour to stay,
the place that sheltered you,
a bit of unintended fire.

Naming the Light

My beautiful brother opens the garage door
on a Saturday morning, taking out the tools
to rake the leaves around the gated house.

He hates this job but does it anyway,
the way he makes his breakfast before daylight.
He gets up as my father would, without question.

The idea of infinity haunts me. The dark days boundless.
My brother raking the leaves on an autumn day
equals the loneliness I feel, waking up

on my mattress, the light not light yet.
My brother that comes in from the cold now
is the same brother that came in from the snow

20 years ago, pounding his boots to wet the carpet,
pieces of frost clinging to his winter hat. Taking off
his gloves, he lets the house warm him. The idea

of the present is that we will last, or that the minutes
might outlive us, that the universe within each
veined leaf will surpass the present tense.

When evening comes, lights dim from each window.
A figure stands by a lamp just about to shut it.
In this moment, it seems as if this job is important,

that if the light fades it will be one less marker of the night.
I realign the pens on my desk as if realigning the stars.
My brother once put his name on a slip of paper.

In his boyhood hand, he wrote his name, *Vincent,*
in script, the slanted letters uncertain and fragile.
Today, I found his name in my pocket.

Ambient Flight

*What flight pattern exists inside the bird? What maps are built
into its wingspan, its air charts, its speed? Will the branch be strong enough
to hold a feathered weight?*

You opened a bird. Unbelievably thin-skinned. Grass wren
fitting perfectly into the pocket of a nest. I want to ask you
to love me in a way that makes me ashamed, as if in asking,
the body becomes burdened. I remove my mask.
Bending to the night, black feathers catch a wind.
The way you call me: a whistle, air dissipating, instinctual.

&

I found a radio and attached it to my bicycle.
I collected sounds: *cracked bell, falling stone, swooping.*
Pieces of music that never existed. The radio transmitted
static wingbeats broken in mid-flight. There was a parade
to celebrate the frayed pieces, like the dead talking
in half syllables, whispers cutting the bright world to pieces.

&

Bats release themselves from branches like plums.
The leaves fall wet with worry, for the final time.
Driven forward, you search for your home,
just a darker boxed shadow within shadow.
Miles of air ahead of you. Look back to see
the wilderness closing in like a canopy, trees
releasing a bundle of leaves from their wild, uncertain arms.

&

I was born with a tender encasing meant to open.
My robe was translucent like skin about to break.
The tiny package of my body was pressed down.
The heart taps an erratic drumbeat. The body is lunatic.

&

A blue egg incubates inside the pocket of an old woman.
Speckled, warm, lint stained. The egg breathes. The oval shape
is the arched bridge she crosses. Albumen coats a body more fragile
than weak. A bird breaks through with its egg teeth, hatching
from a center where nothing was there before it. She holds
the wet bird to her cataract eye, the bird exhausted,
heaving. Science says it will die without its mother,
miniature avian eye opening and shutting.

The bird and the woman both half blind. Both look out as if to see.

&

He leaves. Instantly, without warning,
the thawed swallows vanish into low clouds.
I know so much my hand trembles
and tips over a cup. There's a coldness
in my fingers. A crest is the curve of the breast
that invented breathing. Plumes sever skin
to make the wing fashioned for escape.

&

The wingspan of the color blue thrashes against a tree, red
    tumbles down
with a dead weight.

The man walks toward the tree with a wheelbarrow, to catch
    the heaviness that falls.
But there was no man, no tree,

no fruit spilling down.

☙

I must admit I opened each egg to see
a tragedy inside that fueled song. Everything that I owned
was held hostage in my beak.

My tiny utterances. The words I wasted.

Easter

The F train moves slowly on Sunday and no one
knows the presence of God in the flickering light,
except the woman in a violet dress, hushed into
a lovely bruise, a long stalk of willows in her arms.

No one knows the moment God chooses
to come in the form of Chinese characters
raining down the pages of a book, gently held
by the man sitting next to me.

Twins sit across from me, two Indian men
dressed in matching blue uniforms, whispering
something of their simultaneous unease. Duplicate
voices, Siamese cadence. No one knows the time,

the hour of when and where we're rushing.
The windows of the train have been cracked
with stones or with fists. The criss-crossing
pattern of silver tape masks the damage

like a blister, a star. We are populating
a civilization, singing into the air,
as if into the ear of someone great
or anyone who will listen.

Withholding

Before I gave up everything
I thought of the heat heavy
in the tropics. I kept going
because the light brought me there.
We moved in a locomotive, signs
in yellow, opera of palms, hard bread.
We left the year I fainted.

My eyes sought out strangers.
I am the only one in the car
without a baby. I can say this
in seven dialects. Nightwalks.
Picking out names for our children
made of steam. Riding backwards.
Out the window animals are racing
for their mate. There is the act
of communion and tug of seaweed.
Then rocks ravaged by fire.
There is a voice through the narrow
streets. I am spellbound by that
singular sound. It is a boy.

My soul can abandon
this train. This landscape
a painting with your name etched
onto its back. I begin to begin.

You are something I think of
in my sleep: soul sitting in a room
the size of a beetle. I'll call you
the rough translation of myself:
the beauty about to happen.

Inquiry of Sciences

The anatomy is a difficult thing to study. There is no need
    for you, no room
in the vast equations of my life. There are mistakes and the
    smallest cactus
is dying on the ledge, the shape and size of candy.

Father, there are possible solutions. Theories of love plus X
    minus the square root
of a heavy-handed question mark or blossom. Length of time
    equals the way the boy
touched my skin, the sure signs of life in the path he chose
    in moving down my legs.
Where will it lead? Places to be found: a railroad station,
    a gravel road,
a field where moths loom around the extremities of his face.

In the summer of the year 2000, my father wakes me
    from sleep.
I have not thought of him sufficiently in months. Songs inside me
    are new ones.
Please be new ones. There's a kind of air coming in. Is it sweet?

Your paintings live inside of me.
The bird with a damaged skull, the bird that lays eggs
    into the night. The world
has flesh wounds. I cannot remedy any of this. Inside
    your painting
there is a laughing face, remnants of the five senses, a word
    on a tongue,
sour and inscribed, a mouth with baby teeth growing.

And I kissed the boy until I lost sight of my vocabulary, distance
and logic.

I am placing myself in danger all the time. Before you leave me,
answer this:
How do I live with what I know? Who will be the last one
to love?

Journal of the Diabetic Father

I.

I'm a stack of newspapers.
A kettle. A plate left out to dry.
Scanning the classifieds,

I lose myself in the alphabet.
Falling asleep between the letters,
black print stains my eyes.

II.

My mother wears paper roses in her wig.
Winter, in the kitchen, mice eat their way
through air to reach a nest of bananas.

There is nothing to do but let them go.
She tells me to talk to no one.
I talk to no one. Once I reach the roof

I read a Cantonese mystery.
The children below run,
breaking the windows with sticks.

III.

They call my father King of Burned Pots
as he stands before columns of dishes
in the back of the restaurant,

his arms immersed in brown water,
pork grease and mussel shells.
Hidden behind a veil of white steam

he is washing, always washing.
And I imagine the width
of his tired shoulders.

IV.

I'm under the sink fixing a leak.
Tap water slides across my wrist:
chicken fat, hair, water.

The wrench falls out of my grasp.
The disease has taken me
not by the throat but the hands.

V.

Could there be anything better
than transforming myself
into a boat or a komodo dragon,

forgetting my sickness
and gorging on a bowl of ice cream
and the hundred cashews I adore?

The room smells of alcohol, Tiger Balm,
dried rags. I am sick in the knees.
A cup of rice and a prune for breakfast.

Unemployment has me cooking
the broad beans, overwatering
the rhododendrons, flapping

my slippers on the basement steps.
Lord, no one is listening to me.
The grocer changes beef prices daily.

VI.

My sons are tapping on my door in a dream.
All of them wait for me in a plush corridor.
My wife dresses me in fine trousers.

I'm laughing in front of a long table
of turkey and apples. When I wake,
the house is vacant.

VII.

The sugar is taking effect.
It is burning me up, raising my ashes
to the god I wish I could be.

All over my body
an atlas of wounds, my mouth
a street corner, a reservoir.

Ascension

After checking his pockets
for nickels and dimes, she rubbed
wet cloth upon cloth
until the dirt drifted like a gray spill

of floating cells, faintly alive, bubbling up
for her pruned fingers to touch.
That same year I was baptized.
I drank Holy water from a marble dish,

licked the droplets off my fingers.
Then I took the wafer in my mouth,
letting it shrivel before landing
in my stomach like a divine bullet.

She took his rosary beads from a hook
by the mirror and placed them inside
the dresser among pushpins, unworn
scarves, tubes of chalky lipstick.

She had stopped saying her prayers.
After morning mass, she'd wait for me
across the street. Nights. She locked the door
to the washroom, holding herself steady

over a sink. Her tears dripped into the rust-caked
valves. Mother washed him well when he died.
She cleaned the places that one could easily
forget: the backs of his knees, his chafed heels,

the soft spaces between his legs. She even scoured
the inside of his mouth with a child's toothbrush.
By then his body had gone completely to bone.
I think of the Christ I saw in watercolors

in Catechism books all the Sundays of my life.
How I studied His body, the way it shined
when He was removed from a tilted cross.
Even as He lay twisted and naked, His spine

spiraling to the mud there was a cluster
of red-winged angels reaching toward Him
from the ledge of a cloud and how Mary,
His mother clung to the mortal shell, her lips

sinking into His collar bone, fingers tightening
around the blue face as His soul stormed
over the ladder of His ribs.

The Burning

"... I've lived without names ..."
                    — *Stephen Kuusisto*

Off a seashore in Russia I run, laughing
at the mystery of movement in the form
of water, laughing at my father with sand
on his face who will one day die.

Or imagine for a minute a locomotive
full of people, rocking with the motion
of a vintage sorrow, heads bowing as if
time has beaten them. In my winter season

I think of monks in Penang who sit without
sound for weeks. How they live inside silence.
The silence is alive. The ringing of a bell
is an intricate acorn; my soul hits the ground

when it falls. The apple for all its perfection
will never change. The seed I swallow fashions
a knot in my throat; the fiber of the peel winds
like a staircase leading me down. I look

at my teeth-marks in fruit, in flesh
like a message, an erotic code deciphered
by tearing and biting down. I want to keep
this braille, this transcript of my soul:

My body is a vessel of wanting.
My body is a vessel of fury.
My body is a vessel of apology.

I am the thread & the damage the thread made after the mending.

I am the god I don't know & the fire that burns with no fuel.

Stain

I read of Ali's Kashmir, his country falling
beneath an elephant's foot, the heaviness
that breaks the dry ground and the high cry
of an impending siren. I want to tell everyone
of my alarm. That I am afraid for them.
We must all admit what we fear in the lush
hazard of the waking heart, for what it wants
is to rest, a red flag hidden in uncertain
camouflage, to disappear inside a stupor fog.

For

vacuous plains, for hands, for my empty hands, their possibilities.

For the words I forget, in darkness, for longing that keeps me awake.

For those who are sane, for those who keep it between rock and worm.

For forgetting. For road kill, for the conversations that were half dead,

half breathing. For the solemn girl beneath the tree. For the sparrows

about to scatter. And for her fleshy finger that follows their flight.

For the enemy that is me. The well water runs through my fingers.

This feeling has no name. I want to give it a name. The body wants

what it can't have. It leaps out of its skin to get it. Rain on sand.

Rain on the slope from which I am slipping. For vanishing light.

For perfume, for tinny tunes on the radio. For small tortures, for

your flesh. For all that we rescued. The dormant leaves sprout again.

Letter to a Stranger

After Thomas James

Dear Father,

I drifted on the bouquet of your red tongue
for two years. It was a kingdom, the stadium
of your face. I took sweets from a sealed jar
when mother wasn't looking. I grew up on the back steps
of St. Mary's where I learned to scream at kitten boys
that didn't do what I said. We took the body and the blood
in time. It is possible to be divine in one afternoon.

A girl kneels on pebbles to feel the roughness that will change
her destiny.

When you died, Vincent started his fascination with glass:
its world of definites. Cut or uncut. Severed or whole.
It is the year 2000 and all our failures are tangible.
Vincent is 30 and carries a pistol wrapped
in a powder-blue handkerchief. He will use it
on the clocks, the countenances of apples, the delicate house
of some girl's throat still dripping with wine.

Let me sleep now, in the shelter, in the halt. Stop.

At your burial, I dropped carnations into the big earth.
Mother pulled me along by the sleeve. Now
there is the sound of great thunder as the brothers
come running through the house, their boots cracking
the surface of things, *fuck you's* dropping from their fat lips.

One organ persists alone. Three notes repeating and repeating.

I am governed by terror, sleeplessness, nostalgia.
Mother of God helps me out with my daily chores.
I capture heat in a rusted pot, smooth the bed sheets
with a hammer, take up the hours with my veined hands.
Father, there are magnificent shadows engraving themselves
onto the dinner table. I keep thinking that you are telling me
to go. Let me sleep and dream of the falling architecture
of this house, transform it into an imitation of heaven.
My eyes are closed, two razors.

Dear Father, What kind of music is coming from me? What kind?

Tina Chang's poems have appeared in *Indiana Review, The Missouri Review, Ploughshares, Quarterly West,* and *Sonora Review,* among others. Her poems have been anthologized in *Identity Lessons* (Penguin Putnam, 1999) *Poetry Nation* (Vehicule Press, 1998), *Asian American Literature* (McGraw-Hill, 2001) and *Asian American Poetry: The Next Generation* (University of Illinois Press, 2004). She has received awards from the Academy of American Poets, the Barbara Deming Memorial Fund, the Ludwig Vogelstein Foundation, the New York Foundation for the Arts, *Poets &Writers,* and the Van Lier Foundation, and she has held writing fellowships from Fundación Valparaíso, The MacDowell Colony, the Vermont Studio Center, and Villa Montalvo.